GREAT CLASSIC CARS OF THE WORLD

Cadillac

COLORADO
FAP-82

The luxurious Maybach from Friedrichshafen on Lake Constance was among the most expensive and most technically advanced cars of the 1930s. This SW 38 was provided with an overweight but magnificently equipped body by the Ravensburg coachwork firm of Spohn. Weight: just under three tons, with a 140 bhp, 6-cylinder 3.8 liter engine.

The Ford Model A Roadster was built under license in Germany, England and South America from 1928 to 1931 as a successor to the famous Model T (Tin Lizzy). 4-cylinder engine giving 40 bhp at 2,200 rpm, conventional three-speed transmission and brakes on all four wheels.

The French Delahayes have been known for their advanced engineering and flowing lines since 1895. In 1935 Delage took over the company, after which the Delahaye model 135 coupé with a 6-cylinder engine was developed. The last one was made in 1949; and the bankrupt company taken over by Hotchkiss, who also made tanks.

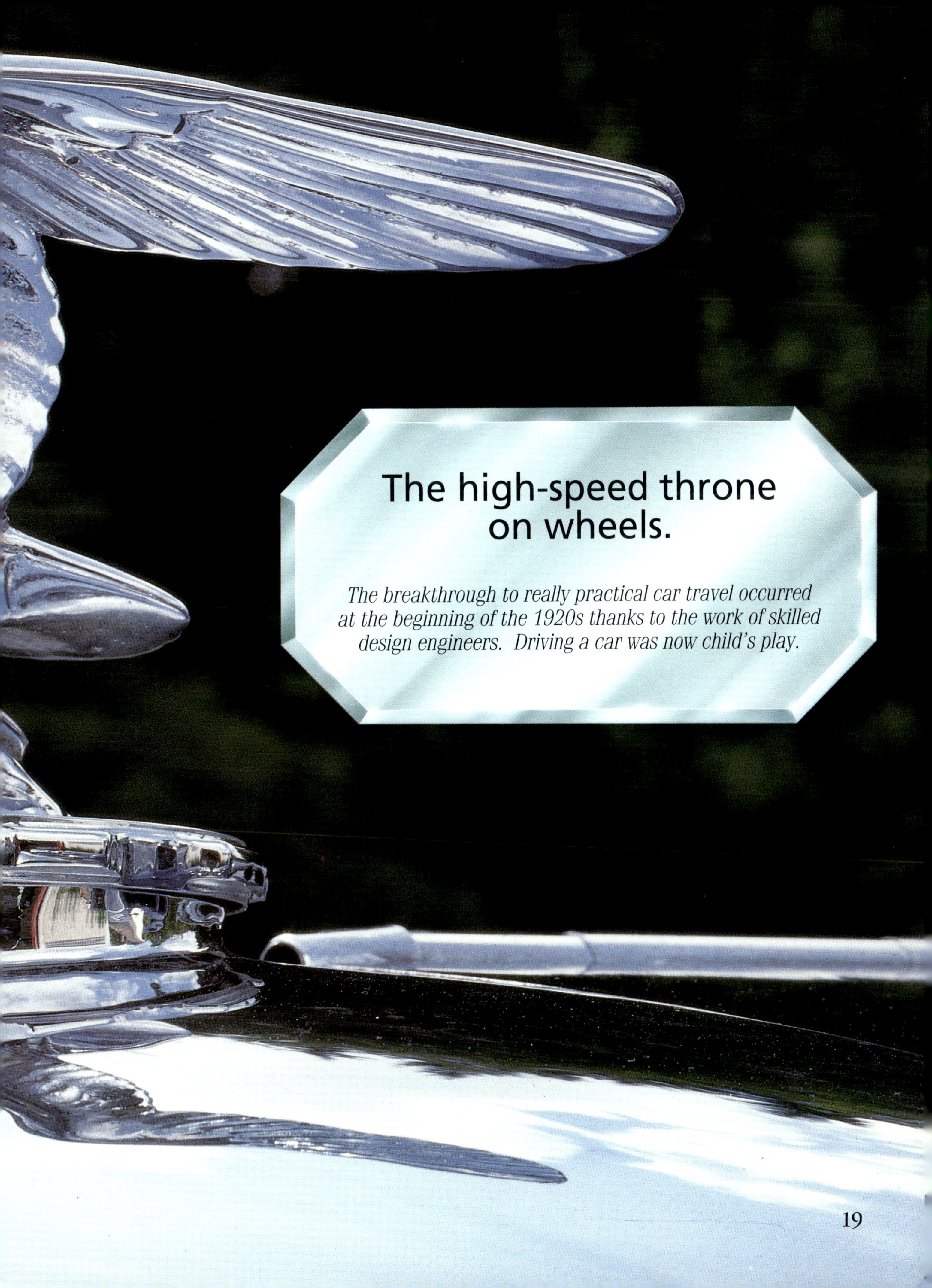

The high-speed throne on wheels.

The breakthrough to really practical car travel occurred at the beginning of the 1920s thanks to the work of skilled design engineers. Driving a car was now child's play.

On 23 December 1904, a joint-venture contract was drawn up between C.S. Rolls and Henry Royce. Exclusivity took priority over quantity, sometimes to the detriment of progress. It was not until 1924 that (servo-assisted) front-wheel brakes were fitted to the last Silver Ghosts. The picture shows a later Phantom II of 1932 (7,688 cc, 120 bhp at 3,000 rpm).

RF 919

The Belgian Minervas figured among Europe's finest and most expensive cars in the 1920s. The silver figurehead on the radiator (left) adorned a 6 ft cylinder sleeve-valve model from 1923 onwards. Precision engineering in a Rolls-Royce Silver Ghost of 1925 (above). Only 6,173 were built between 1906 and 1925.

Count Louis Vorov Zborowski created the three Chitty Chitty Bang Bang racing cars in the early 1920s. The chassis were from pre-World War I Mercedes and the engines from aircraft, varying in capacity from 14,700 cc to 23 liters. The fastest reached speeds of over 125 mph (200 kph) with up to 300 bhp available. The superior picnic basket below is 60 years old, and was sold as a standard accessory in 1922 to Rolls-Royce owners. The photograph shows the modern car created for the film Chitty Chitty Bang Bang, which bears little resemblance to Count Zborowski's cars.

From 1925 to 1935 there were not many changes made to the 7,668 cc six-cylinder engines fitted by Rolls-Royce to their Phantom I and Phantom I (above). Then the V12 Phantom III appeared (1936-1939).

It is the superb details of the luxury cars of the pre-war period which are so fascinating. This Rolls-Royce oil tank with pump was used to thoroughly lubricate chassis and suspension parts every 60 miles.

Ettore Bugatti gained his reputation as one of the world's best automobile designers with this model 23. 1,500 of these were sold between 1914 and 1925. This small 1,496 cc 4-cylinder had 16 valves and an overhead camshaft. This first series production Bugatti was also the most successful.

The first mass-produced automobile in the world was the Model T Ford. 15 million of them were built between 1909 and 1927. This is a 1926 tourer from the first German Ford works in Berlin. There are still 1.8 million of them left world-wide.

-30°
+30°
OB WINTERZEIT
OB SONNENGLUT
VOLTOL
SCHMIERT ALLEMALE GUT
STELLIN
DAS BEWÄHRTE AUTO-BENZIN
MOTOR
ZEISS
Contax
Auto-Richtungszeiger
führt Sie sicher durch den Trubel des Verkehrs
Bezug nur durch den Fachhandel. Ausführliche Druckschriften CONTAX 102 kostenfrei
CARL ZEISS JENA
MOTOR
HANSA
AUTOMOBILE
HOLT KEIN TEUFEL EIN
HANSA-AUTOMOBIL-WERKE AG
VAREL-OLDENBURG-WERKE IN
VAREL-OLDENB. UND BIELEFELD

1920
1929

It was only at the third attempt, in 1908, that Henry Ford made the grade as a car producer. On the right is the Model R Ford of 1907 with Henry Ford sitting next to the driver. The brilliant businessman apparently never owned a driver's license. Gottlieb Daimler also had a chauffeur.

Model T Ford of 1921 (left). Some American States insisted on a special driver's license for Model T Ford drivers, because the two-speed gearshift was pedal-operated. The third pedal was for engaging reverse.

In 1926, Renault set a 24-hour world record with an average speed of 108 mph (173 kph), which in those days was sensational. The huge 6-cylinder engine produced over 200 bhp at 1,500 rpm.

Henry Ford cleverly gained free publicity from feature films and driving stunts. Above, a film scene with Oliver Hardy and Stan Laurel in a Model T Ford of 1913, and on the right a British Model T Ford of 1921 executing a climbing stunt.

The last Model T Ford of 1927, an open tourer costing 480 dollars. The cheapest Model T was offered for 260 dollars in 1923.

Up to 1911, the Model T Ford consisted of wooden bodywork on a strong ladder-frame. Then Ford realized the advantages of sheet metal. Steel sections were used instead of brass frames, which reduced costs and contributed towards the first really cheap automobile. During the first 15 years of production the selling price gradually fell by 590 dollars.

Before the War Fiat also had a loyal clientèle in the luxury car market. They were particularly interested in the powerful touring cars. This Fiat 520, the first with left-hand drive, was very successful. 21,000 were sold between 1928 and 1930. It was the first Fiat sold in Germany.

MARTINI
DER STEIGER

DIE WELT HAT EINEN NEUEN
UND BESSEREN WAGEN
16 Modelle stehen zu Ihrer Verfügung - ein Genie schuf sie, der Zeit vorauseilend - unübertroffen in der Linienführung und Eleganz, einer schöner als der andere - Meisterwerke der Technik
Einer wird bestimmt auch Ihr Typ sein:
Wir zeigen unsere Wagen auf Stand der Intern. Automobil-Ausstellung Berlin
61
NASH
MODELL 1929

Der neue
Maybach
mit Schnellgang

Als andere noch-
im stillen Laboratorium sassen, um die jüngst geborene Glühlampe für das praktische Leben brauchbar zu machen,- da bauten wir schon Automobile! -
Dieser Geist, der vom ersten Tage an die Menschen unseres Werkes beseelte, der immer um eine Spanne voraus ist, hat uns den Weltruf gebracht. Er drückt sich täglich neu in jedem Fahrzeug aus das unser Werk verlässt und er hat unseren Namen zum Inbegriff eines Sondererzeugnisses gemacht,
4 SITZIGES CABRIOLET D. TYP „STUTTGART 260" 10/50 PS
den Namen
MERCEDES-BENZ.
Internationaler Wert zum günstigsten Preis!

These color advertisements appeared at the end of the 1920s in the leading German motoring journal "Motor". It had a modest circulation of 8,000. Stylishly designed drawings linked cars with a fashionable lifestyle. Even then, advertising was simply a subtle form of seduction.

In 1923, the most advanced European sports car was this supercharged Mercedes model 10/40/65 4 cylinders, 2,614 cc and 65 bhp at 2,800 rpm. Top speed was 85 mph (135 kph). A low centre of gravity ensured victory in the big road races, even against cars with greater power. In 1923, Daimler printed his own inflationary money.

50 Milliarden
Gutschein Serie G № 111171
Fünfzig Milliarden Mark
zahlen die Kassen der Daimler-Motoren-Gesellschaft in Stuttgart-Untertürkheim und Sindelfingen gegen diesen Gutschein dem Überbringer. Mit dem Ablaufe des 22. Dezember 1923 verliert dieser Gutschein seine Gültigkeit.
Stuttgart, 2. November 1923.
Daimler-Motoren-Gesellschaft
DAIMLER

IN 1925, ENGLISH HIGH SOCIETY WERE TAKEN ON PICNICS IN ROLLS-ROYCES.

The secret love of screen goddess Greta Garbo was her Phantom I. No other car at that time glided as silently over England's bumpy roads. Naturally the workmanship was vastly superior to that of the Model T Ford which was assembled in about 11 minutes and 40 seconds.

Even conservative-minded people had accepted the car by the early 1920s. Increasingly, horse-drawn carriages disappeared from the street-scene everywhere except in undeveloped parts of the world. After the First World War the automobile became an established feature of society. The well-heeled, however, still made long journeys in the luxurious comfort of Pullman trains, and the rich booked passages on round-the-world cruises in the offices of Thomas Cook.

Travelling by car was no pleasure on the bumpy, dusty cross-country roads. The first Greyhound buses took a full three weeks to make the journey from New York to San Francisco. In winter, many passengers took five weeks to get there. The journey by sea on a luxury steamer via the Panama Canal took ten days and therefore saved time and was infinitely more comfortable than that by car or overland bus. Nevertheless, nothing could halt the progress of the automobile.

Many inventions from that period of euphoric and explosive development are famous, but many are long forgotten. In business you have to blow your own trumpet so the dynamic automobile industry of today likes to give its potential customers that great feeling of being able to own something really valuable and unique. Many so-called "pioneering" innovations of the modern era are clearly old hat. The following description of a few clever refinements in automobile engineering of that period shows how amazingly close they were then to solving today's problems. Take cutting out a certain number of cylinders, for example. As early as 1905, three cylinders in the American 6-cylinder Sturtevant could be put out of action. In the 1917 12-cylinder Enger, six cylinders could be switched off, and in the 1930 8-cylinder Cadillac, four cylinders could be cut out temporarily.

The most difficult problem before the invention of synchromesh gears was the gear shift. This did not affect the drivers of Premier cars, one of over 100 innovative American automobile companies who built passenger vehicles under their own name. By 1920, the four forward speeds could already be preselected electrically. The later Maybach DS8 Zeppelin had preselection of gears on the steering column, which engaged semi-automatically by means of a hydraulic system - entirely without the operation of a clutch, but with three additional reverse gears. (More on this on pages 100 to 105).

The 1914 to 1922 Owen Magnetics were equipped with "fully automatic" gears. The petrol engine drove a generator and the actual motive power was then provided by an electric motor which operated continuously. The luxury car firm conveniently advertised it, therefore, with the catchy slogan "The car of a thousand speeds". The first fully automatic hydraulic transmission was installed in the 1940 Oldsmobile and called the Hydramatic.

Automobile design engineers also took brake technology in different directions. The American Hudson was equipped with hydraulic and additional mechanical four-wheel brakes by 1927. Moreover, from 1912 to 1954, Hudson clutches were cork-lined and ran in an oil-bath.

By 1909 the British Daimler, and by 1911, the Amplex cars from Indiana ran without conventional valves, but with a system of sleeves. This was a development which was later used in the French Voisin in the 1920s and 30s and is again being used experimentally in a 12-cylinder racing engine for Formula 1 cars. The owners of an Adams-Farwell from Dubuque, Iowa had to contend with a 5-cylinder engine which turned horizontally around the driving shaft. The individual air-cooled cylinders sat on a big gear ring.

THE ROLLS-ROYCE LEGEND IS STILL NURTURED WITH BRITISH TENACITY.

A good two-thirds of all Rolls-Royce cars supplied before the Second World War are still in fine condition. This is a line-up of pre-War cars at a rally.

Who today remembers that the first safety-glass with metal wire inserted was used in the 1925 Rickenbacker? The constructors of the 1924 Columbia Six are regarded as the "inventors" of the first thermostatically controlled cooling system. The Waterless Knox from Procupine managed without water-cooling altogether. There were hundreds of thin spacers fitted between the six cylinder walls which dispersed the heat of the engine.

The Oldsmobile people were the first to use chrome on their 1925 model. In 1926, the long-forgotten Apperson was equipped with an electric heater with a fan to keep the interior at a comfortable temperature (slogan: "The eight with eighty less parts").

The following story demonstrates how quickly historic firsts are forgotten. In 1950, Rambler brought out the first safety-belts fitted as standard, which were simply rejected by customers. Rambler went bankrupt. A year later, Chrysler and Buick introduced the first power steering as standard equipment, which is taken for granted today. It was criticized at the time by the famous do-it-yourself magazine "Hobby": "All feeling for the road is lost. Let us hope that this invention will soon disappear". For those technically less-gifted, it's a blessing that the publicity gimmick of the famous Sears store chain did not take off. Their Sears Special was sold in a crate and delivered free of charge to any American railway station. The owner had to assemble the car himself. Sometimes it was the little inventions which provided greater safety and comfort. The 1914 Studebaker was the first to be equipped with a fuel gauge on the dash. Prior to that, fuel consumption had been checked with a dipstick or sight glass. The 1915 Packard pampered the driver with the first air filter with filter cartridge refills. Packard were very sure of themselves: "Ask the man who owns one".

With an eye to safety, the Westcott Automobile Works in Springfield, Ohio created the first bumpers fitted as standard at the front and rear of the car in 1915: "The car with a longer life". But the firm still went bankrupt in 1925.

Prior to 1920, there were 1,218 makes of petrol-driven car, 124 steam car manufacturers and 84 electric car makers in America. Several achieved world fame, but most are long-forgotten. By 1915, one million Fords had seen the light of day, whereas Chevrolet did not achieve the one million mark until 1949.

In the mid-1920s, a new American automobile firm was being launched nearly every day. Sometimes there was

a famous name behind it. This is how the La Salle at Cadillac, the Jewett at Paige, the Marquette at Buick, the Ajax at Nash or the Roosevelt at Marmon all came into being. The Oldsmobile workforce assembled the Viking, and the famous Erskines are a Studebaker product. The Cleveland and Hudson were built by Chandler and Walter Chrysler's cars were sold as Maxwell Chalmers until 1924/25. The world depression at the beginning of the 1930s, however, ensured there was a wholesale clearout among American automobile manufacturers. Prominent names like Franklin (1934), Gardner and Hupmobile were left by the wayside. Production of Kissel Speedsters and luxury limousines was halted in 1931, because at that time most American drivers could only dream about owning a Kissel, or even a Marmon with its 16 matt-painted cylinders, 200 gently purring horsepower and enough torque to allow smooth acceleration from 10 to 105 mph (15 to 170 kph) in top gear. Most of the jewels of the American car industry perished during this period. The survivors were the well-made, middle-of-the-road makes.

Splendour and Misery of the 1930s

In America between 1931 and 1938 were built the magnificent automobiles of the classic era. The air-cooled Franklin was considered a technological sensation.

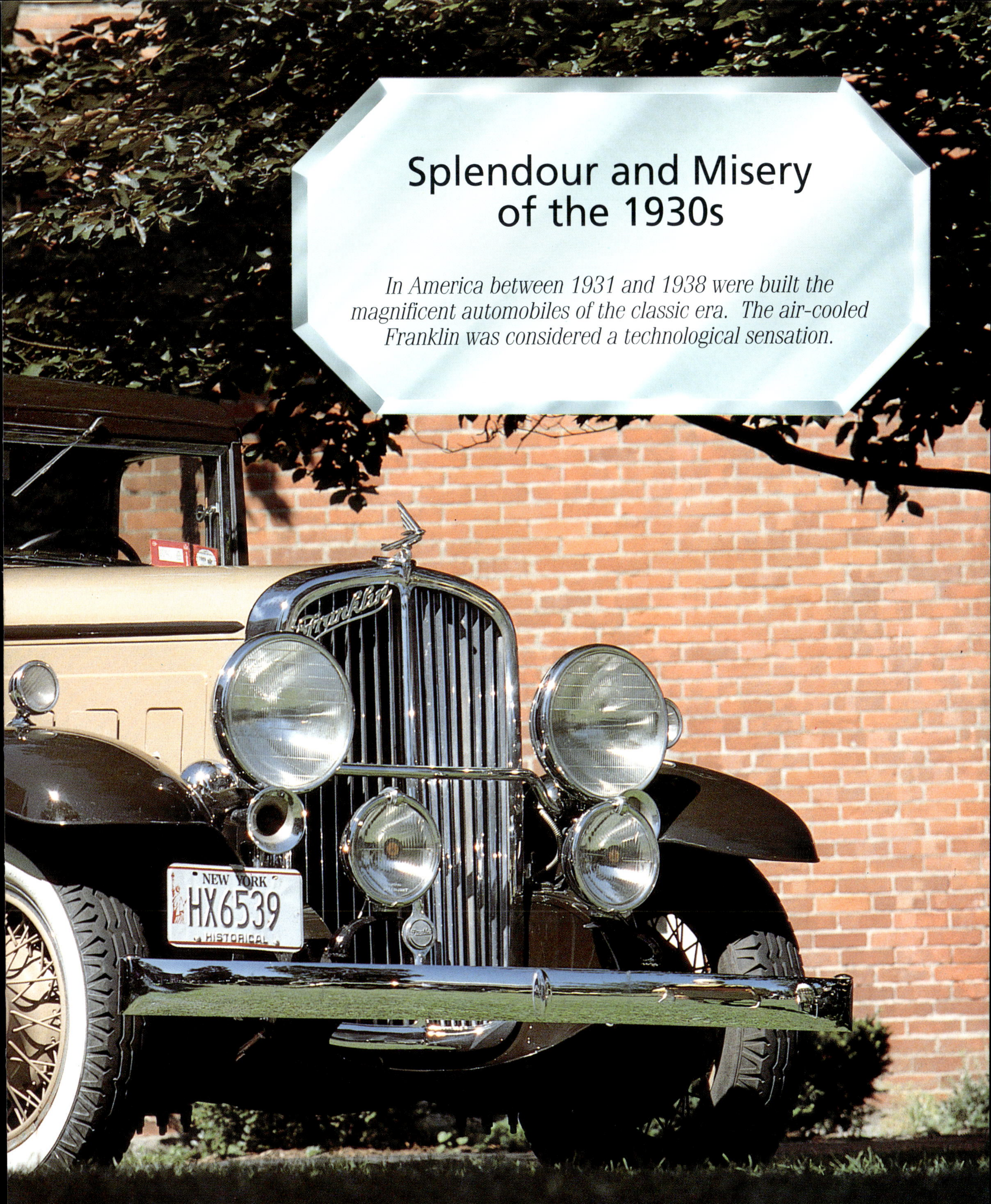

The air-cooled Franklins were built in Syracuse near New York from 1902 to 1934. The company relied upon the élite. Customers included airplane manufacturer Donald Douglas and aviator Charles Lindbergh. Pictured here is the 12-cylinder with bodywork by Le Baron.

The famous 6-cylinder Franklin engines are all air-cooled. The Olympic gave 100 bhp at 3,100 rpm and 80 mph (130 kph). Franklin power units also proved reliable as aircraft engines, after the patents for air-cooling had been taken over by other companies.

Sixty years after its first introduction at the New York Motor Show in 1928, the Duesenberg J still exerts the same fascination. Its 6.9 liter 265 bhp straight eight engine was a good 80 bhp more powerful than the Bentley Speed Six, for example, and also better off than the unbeatable supercharged Mercedes SS sports car with its 225 bhp. Duesenberg was one of the first production cars with four hydraulic drum-brakes.

The 1931 Duesenberg Model J. America's most powerful, expensive and fastest car included details like this perfectly-shaped hood and spare wheel. The car was at that time about forty times more expensive than a Ford A roadster.

This uniquely elegant Duesenberg J was designed in 1929 by Gordon Buehrig. The best coachbuilders then made the final bodywork. Murphy was responsible for the Beverley saloon car. Derham made the Torpedo Phaetons and four-seater tourer models. They were the most expensive cars in the world at the beginning of the 1930s.

The famous American classics were also sold in Germany in small numbers. Here are some contemporary advertisements from the "Motor" journal.

As a rule, Duesenberg supplied coachbuilders with the engine, transmission and chassis. They then created the perfectly shaped bodywork which could be up to 23 ft (7 m) in length. This 1935 Duesenberg Model J, with bodywork by Bohman und Schwartz is irreplaceable. Its value is about 2 million dollars.

H.H. Franklin was adamant that his air-cooled 6-cylinder engines could withstand any stress, and to prove it, this 100 bhp car was driven non-stop from Washington to San Francisco (about 3,000 miles or 5,000 kilometers) in first gear.

By the mid-1930s only a few wealthy Americans could afford a Duesenberg. This model J was fitted out by Derham with modern bodywork. Some Duesenbergs were provided with new bodywork every ten years.

Walter Chrysler spent some years working for various car firms. Then, in 1924 he decided to establish his own business. This 1932 8-cylinder by Le Baron was a great success. Chrysler died in 1940. He was by then the third biggest car manufacturer in America.

Harry C. Stutz is considered the most eminent sportscar manufacturer in America before World War II, followed by Duesenberg. Here is an 8-cylinder Stutz with 4 valves per cylinder, overhead camshaft, 4-wheel hydraulic brakes, top speeds of over 100 mph and Le Baron bodywork.

This 1930 Ruxton is a real rarity. The paintwork is original. Front-wheel drive, Continental straight eight engine, 100 bhp and Budd chassis.

The Marmon V16 was one of the first American 16-cylinder engines, at about the same time as the Cadillac V16. This 1931 model has an output of 200 bhp from 7,917 cc, and is worth a cool million dollars.

The Auburn Speedsters were considered hot stuff in the 1930s. Apart from the 8-cylinder versions, with and without supercharger, there was a 160 bhp V12 by Lycoming (photo). The Auburn Speedster is a trademark of the Auburn Cord and Duesenberg empire of Errett Lobban Cord. In 1937 the group of companies was dissolved.

LAND OF LINCOLN
ANTIQUE
9067
VEHICLE
84 ILLINOIS 85

The 1934 Packard V12 by Le Baron was the epitome of the luxurious touring car, even driven by American presidents. The black Cord L-29 (far left) caused a sensation between 1929 and 1932. Front-wheel drive, top speed over 100 mph (165 kph), a Lycoming FDA straight 8-engine, 125 bhp.

One of the biggest flops in the history of the motor car was the 1934 Imperial Airflow by Chrysler. Technologically, this seven-seater was first-class, but its streamlined shape was too avant-garde for its time.

The Chrysler Newport was used as pace car to lead off the 1941 Indianapolis 500 mile race. It had been developed as early as 1939. With 135 bhp from its straight eight engine, it remained the only example of its kind.

The 1933 V12 Pierce Arrow was hailed as the most modern luxury car in America. It became known as the "Silver Arrow".

The French company Fernandez was designing the most exciting bodywork for American and European customers in the mid-1930s. Above, a 1935 Renault Nervastella, which had a 4.8 liter straight eight engine.

This 1934 La Salle was a particularly advanced design - V8, 120 bhp, press-button starter and handbrake on the left under the dash; a novelty in America. La Salle was a Cadillac subsidiary.

The 1939 Buick Roadmaster was equipped with an electric indicator in the shape of the company logo on the trunk lid. The semi-faired in headlights were considered ultra-trendy and set the style for the "shark" radiator grilles of the 1940s.

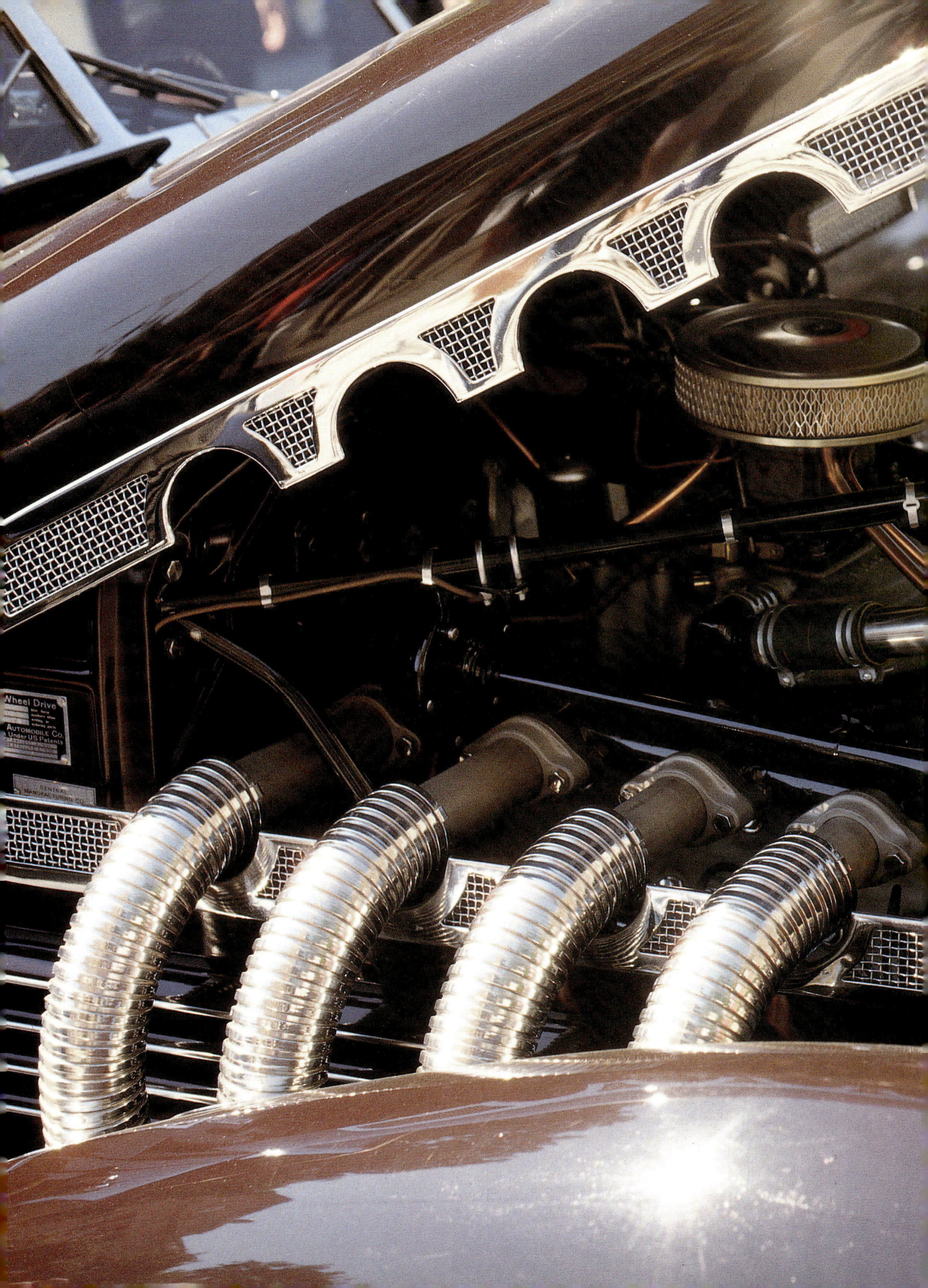
Wheel Drive
Automobile Co.
Under US Patents
Central
Manufacturing Co.

The most technologically daring car of the 1930s, was the Cord 812 with a 125 bhp V8 engine and front-wheel drive. Designed and built by Gordon Buehrig in 1935, it was way ahead of its time. This beautiful 170 bhp supercharged version is recognizable by the outside exhaust pipes.

AMERICA IN THE 1930S MEANT METROPOLITAN FLAIR, ADVENTURE AND FASHION

In 1931 Walter Chrysler's massive Imperial Eight (right) was considered to be one of the most aristocratic of vehicles. Flexible engine mountings, an automatic clutch and optional freewheel made it even more enjoyable to drive.

President Theodore ("Teddy") Roosevelt preferred to drive a Baker electric car. These easy to drive cars were particularly suitable for short journeys and were very popular with women drivers. Another of the president's cars, the mighty White Steam car, offered America's number one the luxury of a continuously variable transmission. For big parades "Teddy" used one of his two Pierce Arrows. In 1909 these represented the sum total of the government's fleet of cars.

By the beginning of the 1930s the American President could choose between 28 distinguished marques. President Hoover chose a car appropriate to his rank - a 16-cylinder Cadillac, type 452 with 185 bhp at 3,400 rpm. His predecessors Harding and Coolidge chose Pierce Arrows with straight 8-cylinder or V12 engines and 150 bhp, which experts considered far superior. There was a notable absence of vibration in the 12-cylinder.

Franklin Roosevelt had a preference for 12-cylinder Packards. His retinue of secret service cars were supplied by Pierce Arrow and were straight eights. In 1933, a Lincoln V12 is mentioned for the first time in contemporary reports as an additional security vehicle.

This was due to Henry Ford's influence on the American government. The largest and most powerful automobile manufacturer in the world wanted to see the American President in a Ford Lincoln. In 1939 the deal was finalized. The White House leased a Lincoln, measuring an enormous 23 ft (7.09 m) in length and 6 ft 9 in (2.05 m) wide. The black monster at 6 ft 4 in (1.94 m) tall towered above the President and his retinue. This Lincoln went down in American history as the "Sunshine Special". The "Sunshine Special", complete with extras, weighed a massive 4.3 tons. The bodywork was hand-crafted by the Brunn company and invoiced at 4,950 dollars. The total cost was 8,348 dollars 74 cents. This was well worth it for the publicity even then. The "Sun-shine Special" remained in the service of the American government until 1950. All presidential cars after this were ordered from Ford.

For political reasons Presidents could not make use of what were in fact the most luxurious and expensive cars of the 1930s. Although the Duesenberg brothers had every last screw of their fantastic luxury cars made in America, they were still considered German immigrants. Apart from the Bugatti Royale, of which only six were built, the Duesenberg Js were the most expensive cars at the time. The basic price for chassis and engine was 8,590 dollars. Around 8,000 to 12,000 dollars more had to be provided for the bodywork. 20,000 dollars bought three Packard V12s or two Cadillac V16s, and the Duesenberg J only had eight cylinders. However, they were enough to cause a sensation in the motoring world, with their 265 bhp, compared with the 150 bhp at most of the 12 and 16-cylinder competition.

In the middle of the worst economic crisis of the time (1932) Duesenberg launched the Model SJ with Roots blower. Its performance data of 320 bhp and a top speed of over 130 mph (205 kph) were out of this world. The basic price for engine and chassis was now 15,000 dollars. The coachbuilder charged as much again for appropriate bodywork. The same amount of money bought 64 Ford coupés with 8-cylinder engines. According to records in the Duesenberg Museum in Auburn, USA, Duesenberg never gave the actual output and top speeds of his models. Performance data known today originates from the engine-makers Lycoming, who supplied the basic power units. At Duesenberg the engines were completed and run in. Duesenberg had the engines run on the bench for almost 100 hours, before engine, transmission and chassis were delivered as a complete running unit to the bodywork manufacturers.

The least powerful Duesenberg Model J of 1928 was road-tested by "Trade Magazine" in December 1928 in a four-seater open tourer version. The two test drivers reached speeds of 89 mph (147 kph) in second gear and 116 mph in third gear. This was not with the windscreen flat to improve the aerodynamics, but with it kept raised, even at this speed, because the ambient

temperature was only eight degrees centigrade and the test drivers were frozen. The absolute top speed was never reached on either of the two straight stretches of road because they were too short. The test car was the first Duesenberg J model, which already had a few thousand miles under its belt.

The later supercharged Duesenberg SJ Speedster effortlessly reached speeds of 130 mph (215 kph) at 4,100 rpm. The Duesenberg SJs were without doubt the fastest, most powerful and also the most expensive production cars of that time. Present auction prices (in 1989) vary between 5 and 10 million dollars, depending on the version.

Technically speaking, the Duesenberg Js and SJs were not superior to the products of the American manufacturers of luxury sportscars and limousines. The supercharged 8-cylinder engine was extremely noisy compared to a 16-cylinder Marmon or Cadillac unit. Accelerating caused the glass to rattle in the window frames. It was a thinly disguised racing engine in a luxurious body.

Since the Duesenberg brothers saw themselves first and foremost as engine designers, they sought new technical solutions. The gear shift consisted of five positions including two neutral positions. There were, therefore, only three forward gears available, which could be engaged in a straight line through a neutral shift channel (not through the usual H-shaped gate). In this way, shifting gears up and down was much simpler. McLaren use a similar system in their Formula 1 racing cars.

A two-stage Schebler carburetor was used for the first time. When ticking over or driving slowly, the mixture of air and fuel is controlled by the first throttle valve. The second throttle valve is activated for acceleration. The engine thus obtains the correct air/fuel mixture according to its needs. Thanks to this carburetor even drivers with little or no experience of racing could handle the massive

The Auburn Speedster was sold with superb build quality at ridiculously low prices. A price of 1,895 dollars, compared to the 4,900 dollars for the Stutz Bearcat, damaged the reputation of the much cheaper Auburn.

power of these engines. Petrol consumption was between 8 and 10 mpg for a 320 bhp engine, which by the standards of those days was not particularly high.

Regular lubrication of the chassis and its linkages, joints, etc was part of normal routine servicing at the beginning of the 1930s. Not every 5,000 miles, but every 100 miles or so. Since there were between 8 and 32 points to lubricate, this dirty work was a far from pleasant activity.

This was not the case with the Duesenbergs. All the J and SJ cars were equipped with centralized lubrication, which was controlled from the dashboard. All the chassis lubrication points were linked to the central lubricating system. The kingpins and even the shock absorber bushes were oiled regularly every 75 miles (123 kilometers) fully automatically.

The oil pump was operated by means of an auxiliary chain drive. The driver could read off the following data on his dashboard: oil pump function OK, oil reservoir full, warning light if empty. After 700 miles, an additional warning light requested an oil change. Another indicator showed the driver the acid level in the 160 ampere hour battery.

But that is by no means all. Duesenberg drivers were informed of their progress by means of a speedometer with an upper limit of 150 miles per hour (240 kph) and a rev counter whose upper limit was 5,000 revolutions. Whereas brake failure in those days was often simply accepted as an act of God, Duesenberg equipped his cars with a brake pressure indicator, so that wear and overheating of the linings could be detected from the dashboard. Finally, an ammeter, a petrol gauge, a central switch for the electrical equipment and an altimeter ensured that the driver could monitor all engine and chassis functions.

The Duesenberg J/SJ was truly one of a kind. Bankruptcy for the firm was virtually built into it. There were only 36 of these unique cars sold, the last, in 1937, to an Indian Maharajah. Then the lights went out in the yellow brick building in Auburn. It was the end of an almost unreal era.

THE VALUE-FOR-MONEY AUBURN SPEEDSTER ESTABLISHED MANY LONG-DISTANCE WORLD RECORDS.

Auburn attributed to his Speedsters the speed of an aircraft, the luxury of a yacht and the comfort of a couch. The golf clubs were housed in a separate compartment in the trunk. Most of the Auburn Speedsters bought were open cars. Marlene Dietrich among others had a Sunny California.

Battleship on four wheels

Crowned heads of state rode in armoured state coaches in the 1930s, such as this 1935 Mercedes 770 belonging to the Japanese emperor Hirohito.

Racing car technology in a production car. The 8-cylinder 540 K Special Roadster impresses through its power (160 bhp) and its ideal combination of sporting character and luxury. Above (inset) is an SSK racing engine, and on the right (inset) is the dashboard decorated with mother-of-pearl.

Daimler-Benz introduced the first standard rear-engined production car at the 1934 Berlin Motor Show. This Model 150 Sports Roadster was developed in 1935 for the "2,000 Kilometer Rally", at that time the most important German reliability trial. 4 cylinder, 1,498 cc engine, 55 bhp, 87 mph (140 kph). The Model 150 was mid-engined, for better weight distribution.

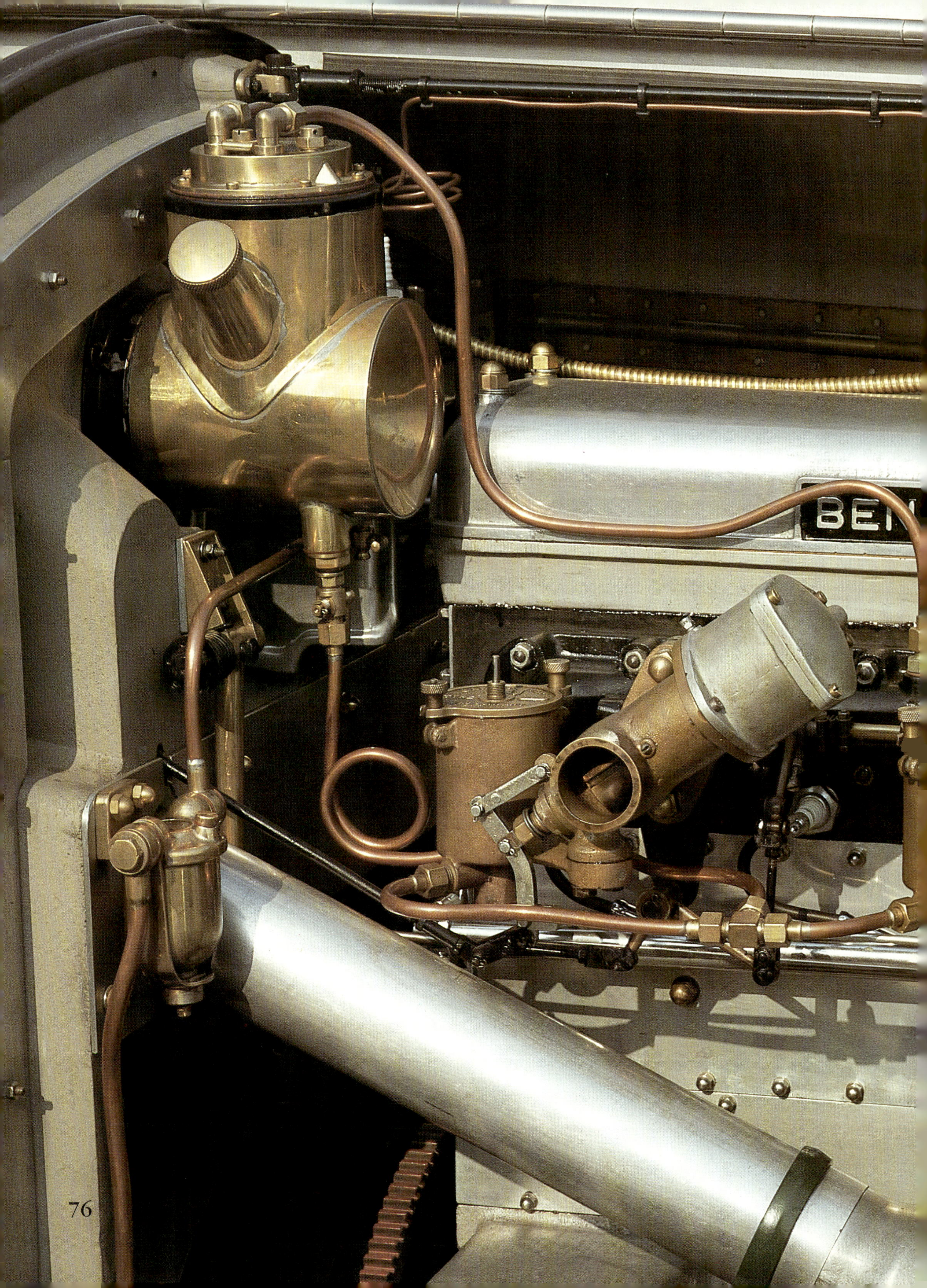
BEN

The Bentley 4.5 liter 4-cylinder sports-racing engine, extremely reliable over long distances, won nearly every important sports car race from 1927 to 1931. It gave 100 bhp at 3,500 rpm, with compression of 5.1:1, and 4 gears. The 2 SU carburettors had bronze bodies. Only 665 of these cars were sold.

No other English firm pursued international long-distance success so intently as Walter Owen Bentley and his legendary "Bentley Boys" racing team. Five Le Mans victories emphasized the robustness of this 2.5 ton machine. Here is a 1931 4.5 liter model.

2me GRAND PRIX
AUTOMOBILE
MONACO
6 AVRIL 1930
ROLLS-ROYCE
& BENTLEY
TLEY

BMW did not start automobile production until 1928, selling a version of the English Austin Seven with great success under license as the BMW Dixi. In 1934, this Type 315/1, a 6-cylinder with 40 bhp and a top speed of 75 mph (120 kph), was the ideal sports car for the private owner (main photo). It achieved overall victory in the international Alpine Rally against supercharged cars which were five times more powerful. The almost unbeatable BMW 328 was developed in 1938 from the 315.

The 1932 3 liter Lagonda Sports Tourer (far left) is British through and through. Lagonda won the 24-hour Le Mans race in 1935. From 1933 onwards, the famous Maybach preselector transmission was used in some 3 liter Lagondas (3,181 cc, 6-cylinders, and 120 bhp. Lagonda was bought by other firms on more than one occasion, finally being merged in 1947 with Aston Martin. The most powerful engine of the 1930s classic English sports car era is this rare 8-liter Bentley (left). It was a 6-cylinder with 7,982 cc, 225 bhp and a top speed of 105 mph. One hundred of these were supplied between 1930 and 1932.

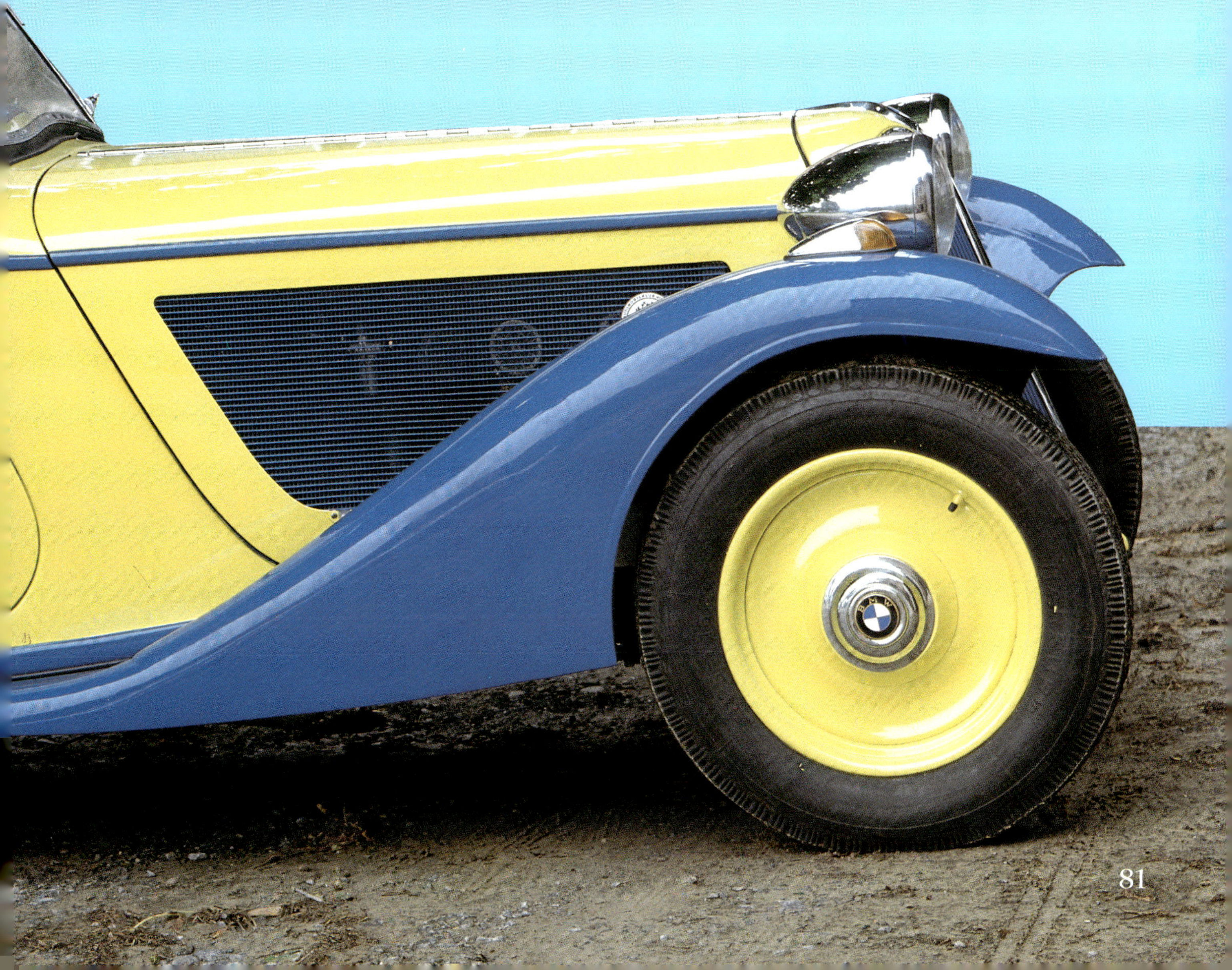

From 1930 onwards, nearly all German car firms experimented with streamlined bodywork. This Mercedes model 320 "motorway courier" was developed in 1938 and was sold at that time for 9,000 marks. It had a 3.2 liter straight 6-cylinder engine, giving 78 bhp and speeds of about 85 to 90 mph (135 to 145 kph). In 1938, Daimler-Benz had eight totally different model ranges. They varied from the 170 H rear-engine car, via the middle of the range front-engined cars, to the racy 540 K sports roadster and the huge model 770 known as the Großer Mercedes.

Bugatti Royale - the biggest and most expensive car in the world. Only six of them were built between 1929 and 1933. They fetch 16 to 20 million dollars at today's auction prices. The 12.7 liter engine units were later used in railcars by the French railway.

No two Hispano Suizas were alike. Each part was hand-crafted, and owners were therefore provided with a detailed list of the craftsmen responsible for, say, the left or right front wing. The hard steel was worked into shape for days on end over a wooden block. The use of filler was unheard of in 1938, when this 220 bhp 12-cylinder was built.

Together with Maybach and Mercedes, Horch was a by-word for stately limousines and sports cars in the 1930s. This Horch model 830 BK drophead coupé was developed by engineer Paul Daimler, the son of Gottfried Daimler and represented the ideal synthesis of power and elegance. It had the first German V8 engine of 3,517 cc, giving 75 bhp.

Radiator of the Horch 780, a quality design from Zwickau.

Delahaye were the first European firm to manufacture detachable cylinder heads. This 6-cylinder from the 135 range was fed by large twin carburettors and gave 130 bhp from 3,557 cc. Delahaye also developed 12-cylinder engines with a capacity of 4.5 liters.

This Delahaye 135 was developed at the end of the 1930s and sold until 1949. The bodywork was flamboyant for the 1930s. But this could not prevent the demise of one of the most renowned French marques. Post-war tax laws made life impossible for French luxury car firms.

Finest quality - the interior of a Hispano Suiza J12. Total Hispano Suiza production from 1931 to 1938 was about 8,750. Below is a flamboyant Delahaye Cabriolet. About 25,000 Delahayes were manufactured between 1895 and 1954.

One of the fastest pre-War sports cars in the 1100 cc class was this Fiat Balilla 508S with a 995 cc engine and 36 bhp. Around 1,200 Balilla 508 S cars were sold in total.

1930 1939

Wilhelm Maybach was considered "King of the automobile designers" by the French. As a friend and collaborator of Gottlieb Daimler, he was the genius who created the first Mercedes which became the model for the modern automobile. Wilhelm Maybach is often described as being the creator of the Maybach luxury car. In actual fact, it was his son, Dr Karl Maybach, who founded the Maybach engine manufacturing company in Friedrichshafen in 1910, and built those absolutely world-class cars which were the acme of technical perfection in the 1930s.

MAYBACH, THE GEM FROM THE PROVINCES. AS EXPENSIVE AS 33 OPEL P4S.

Those who drove a Maybach in the 1930s did not worry about the fuel consumption. They had to be extremely well off to start with, since the Maybach Zeppelin was Germany's most expensive car. The Maybach SW 38 Cabriolet was made exclusively to order. The bodywork was by Spohn in Ravensburg.

Maybach owners had to be prepared to pay almost double the purchase price of the Großer Mercedes, the Horch or the Wanderer. Around 1930, Maybach charged 34,000 marks for the rolling chassis alone. The coachbuilder wanted another 15,000 to 20,000 marks. Approximately 300 Maybach 12-cylinder Zeppelins were built. It was the most expensive car in Germany, and also in the world, apart from the six Bugatti Royales and the Duesenbergs. For 50,000 marks you could buy 33 Opel Olympias or 5 Dornier holiday houses on Lake Constance.

The wealthiest industrialists drove Maybachs, and politicians also found

they suited their need for dignified transport. Baron Thyssen, Werner von Siemens, baking product manufacturer Oetker, steel producer Hoesch, and even the Deutsche Arbeitsfront Berlin (= German Labour Front in Berlin), a predecessor of the Trade Unions, and the Eidgenössische Postverwaltung (= Swiss Postal Administration) ordered the expensive Maybachs. Hitler's powerful deputies, notably Goebbels, Himmler and Keitel, also drove around in the 30s in Maybach DS8s with 8 liter 12-cylinder engines giving 200 bhp.

Although Karl Maybach only regarded his aristocratic cars as good publicity for the firm ("The real money comes from the sale of our railcar engines"), the Maybach was streets ahead of its rivals in ease of operation. The limousines, which weigh up to 3.5 tons, can be effortlessly slipped into gear by gently pressing two levers on the steering wheel with the thumb. To shift into a higher gear, the left hand preselector lever is pressed upwards; by taking the ft briefly off the accelerator the next gear is engaged, without using a clutch. Maybach justifiably claimed, "Four noiseless (!) gears, which, functioning in the manner of electric switches and not requiring a clutch, can be conveniently controlled from the steering wheel". Operation of the gear shift from the steering wheel was by pneumatic power, the necessary vacuum being generated by the engine. The so-called 1A gear and reverse could be engaged via a central gearshift lever in conjunction with the ft clutch. If the preselector levers on the steering wheel were now operated, the two

gears were sub-divided into a further four gears each. Thus the driver had access to twelve gears. Even now, the Maybach-Zeppelin gearshift functions perfectly in the fifty-year-old cars.

You could easily write a whole book on the technical refinements of the extraordinary Maybach.

Now for some more interesting details. On Maybach cars, the hydraulic jacking system was permanently fitted to the chassis. Today this is a speciality of Formula 1 cars.

Maybach drivers were provided with a type of servo-assistance for the four drum brakes, which were equipped with brake equalizers. The Maybach brake system was known as a vacuum brake and like today's servo brakes only worked with the engine running. An additional mechanical handbrake operated on the rear wheels.

Although Maybach limousines were an impressive size, being almost 20 ft (6 m) in length and 6 ft 1.5 in (1.85 m) wide, the most staggering thing about them was their top speed of 115 to 120 mph (185 to 190 kph), depending on the type of bodywork. The 200 bhp Maybach was an extremely fast touring car for its time.

Maybach drivers required a "Klasse II" driver's license for heavy goods vehicles and omnibuses (before 1933), because the weight of the car exceeded 2.5 tons. After 1933, and at the instigation of the Nazis who wanted to drive Maybachs themselves, Maybach drivers could have their "Klasse III b" driver's license converted to "Klasse II".

After the War, a further handful of Maybachs were assembled from spare parts and completed with "battleship"-style coachwork by Spohn, the Ravensburg bodywork company. Maybach is today MTU, a specialist in large engines, especially for aircraft. The father of the legendary Maybach cars, Prof. Dr Karl Maybach, died in 1960 aged 81.

There are now approximately 30 Maybach Zeppelin 12-cylinder cars and 110 6-cylinders carefully looked after by their owners. This is not surprising,

THE OUTBREAK OF THE SECOND WORLD WAR SIGNALLED THE END OF THE MAGNIFICENT ERA OF COSTLY PRESTIGE CARS.

Hitler's armoured car used for parades and rallies is now an exhibit in the French car museum in Lyons (above). One of the first car radios from 1939 (right). Even beautiful radiator figureheads disappeared into limbo at the end of the 1930s (top)

"The dashboard is the visiting card of a prestige car." Horch designer Paul Daimler, the son of Gottlieb Daimler, followed this principle when he provided this Horch 853 with inlaid mother-of-pearl fittings.

This American Duesenberg with Swiss Graber bodywork has perfect lines. It is a real rarity, worth more than a million dollars.

since auction prices for fine examples have doubled in the last few years. A Maybach Zeppelin would now fetch between 700,000 and 1.2 million marks. Between 1921 and 1940 there were only about 2,300 Maybachs sold. In 1937 and 1938, they formed only 0.1 per cent of German car production.

The exclusivity of these luxury cars was unmistakable even then. Daimler-Benz, their main competitor, supplied at least ten times as many luxury cars in 1937-38 at prices of over 20,000 marks.

In England, 1,767 Rolls-Royce Phantom IIs left the works between 1929 and 1935. Its successor, the Phantom III, was not so successful. Only 717 of these were purchased between 1936 and 1939. Astonishingly, there were 3,827 Rolls-Royce 20/25s sold from 1929 to 1936. Between 1929 and 1939, 6,311 cars were sold off the English Rolls-Royce production lines. This does not include figures for American Rolls-Royce production.

Another technical masterpiece of the 1930s was the 1933 Hispano-Suiza J12 Coupé. The 9,425 cc 12-cylinder engine was considered to be the finest automobile engine in Europe, along with the Maybach 12-cylinder. 220 bhp made possible both a top speed of 112 mph (180 kph) and proven acceleration from 0 to 60 mph in 12 seconds. These are impressive figures for a coupé weighing over two tons. Rolls-Royce were so enthusiastic about this Hispano V12 that they are said to have seriously considered building it under license. Negotiations broke down because of objections by the designer Marc Birkigt and King Alfonso of Spain, whose commitment to the company was not only of a financial nature. The pride of the designer and the monarch prevented any kind of business link with arch-rival Rolls-Royce.

In retrospect we can see that the demise of these uniquely beautiful large classics of the 1930s was predestined. The real money was in economically-priced medium-sized cars such as the Ford Model A Roadster, the Opel Olympia, or the Mercedes 170 and 200. They could be bought for around 4,500 marks in 1937 and satisfied millions of customers.

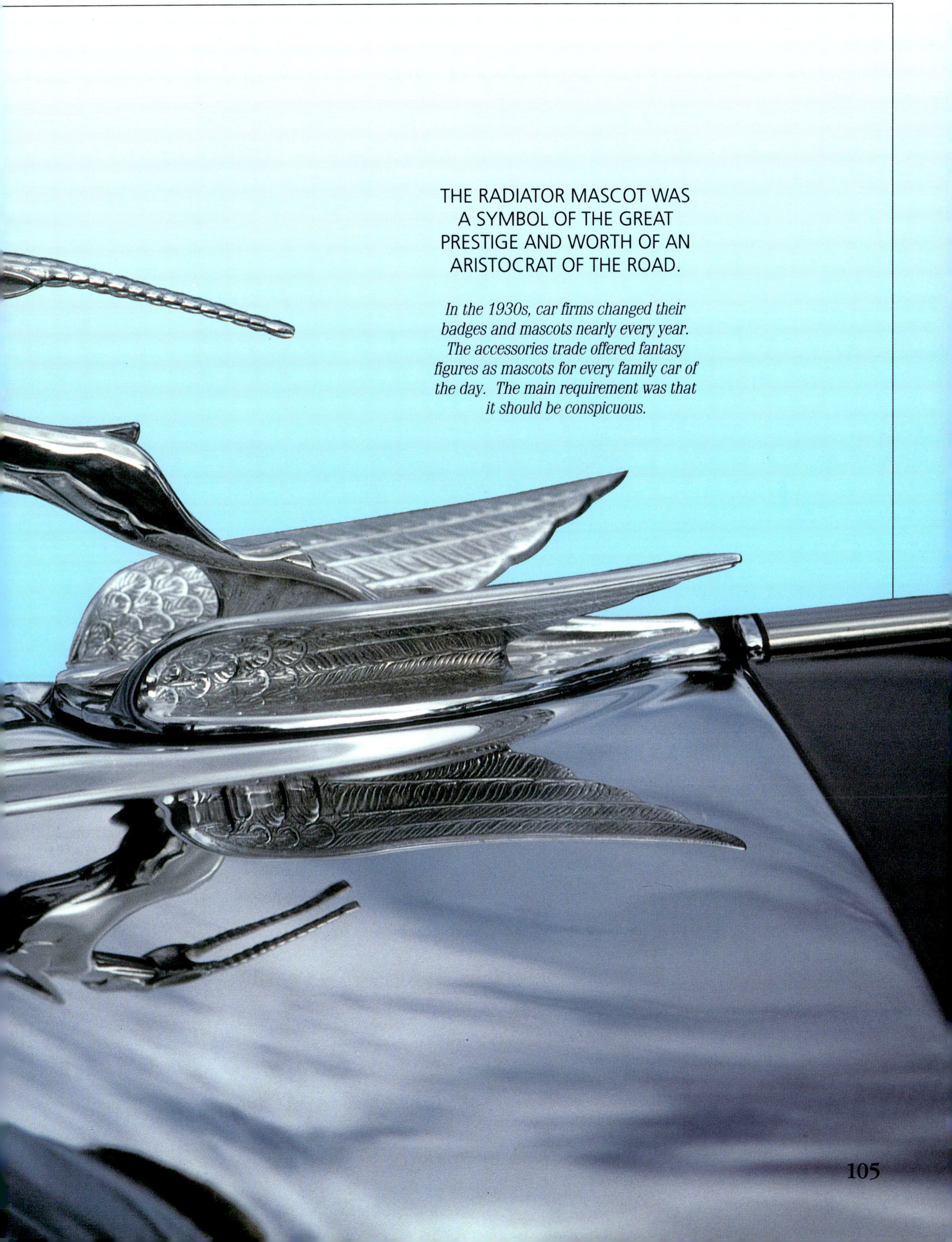

THE RADIATOR MASCOT WAS A SYMBOL OF THE GREAT PRESTIGE AND WORTH OF AN ARISTOCRAT OF THE ROAD.

In the 1930s, car firms changed their badges and mascots nearly every year. The accessories trade offered fantasy figures as mascots for every family car of the day. The main requirement was that it should be conspicuous.

Greetings from 'Jaws'

In the mid-1940s, a shoal of aggressive sharks got their teeth into the wallets of America. The Buick Eight was the craziest of them all.

Super

This shiny chrome interior exuded the sort of luxury that Americans had been forced to do without in the War years, when manufacturers were temporarily forbidden to supply any private cars. This 1948 Buick dashboard shows the exuberance of their renewed prosperity.

DEFROS
PULL
LIGHTER
AIRVEN
OFF

This 1948 Chevrolet Stylemaster was used as pace car for the Indianapolis 500-mile race, an honor for American manufacturers. Chevrolet charged only 1,890 dollars for this 6-cylinder in 1948. Its present value is around 50,000 dollars.

NTERNATIONAL
XXV
FC
1942

President Eisenhower on the drive to the Capitol. The white Cadillac Eldorado was built in 1949/50. On the left is a no less famous 'Sunshine Special' carrying the security men. After the Cadillac interlude, American presidents drove only in Lincolns by Ford.

The yellow 1949 Buick Roadmaster Riviera is recognizable by the four 'bull's eyes' on the front wings. The chrome 'Sweep Spears' trim was specially created for this model.

"More of everything you want with Mercury" was how Mercury advertised the 1949 V8 which gave 95 bhp. It is nowadays a sought-after dreamboat car with unique lines.

200 YEARS
USA

Harley Earl, General Motor's highly individual chief designer, created this 1948 Buick Roadmaster Convertible. The powerful 5.2 liter, 144 bhp, straight 8 engine harmonised perfectly with the new 3 speed Dynaflow transmission. Then: 2,837 dollars. Now: more than 50,000 dollars.

The Graham Hollywood (left, inset) was one of the most sought-after cars of the 1940s. Graham took over the rights to the Cord 812 and sold it under the company name of Hupmobile until 1941. The white 1941 Buick with bodywork by Fisher, was one of the last built with horizontal chrome radiator bars.

296
XF/FL

A 1948 Buick Super four-door sedan, superior than Ford as it was better equipped with technical refinements as an aerial operated from inside, a push-button radio and heated seats. A bargain at 2,087 dollars: today's value is 28,000 dollars.

1940
1949

On closer inspection, the first post-war models from the American car giants were merely re-hashed versions of 1941 models. From 1942 to mid-1945, production in the big car factories was exclusively geared to the needs of the army and air force. Ford became the most profitable aircraft manufacturer in history in these years. The famous Liberator bomber was produced at Ford in huge numbers.

In 1945, the war was over and every American wanted to fulfil his dream of owning his own car. By 1946, one in ten Americans was working either directly or indirectly for the automobile industry because the demand for new cars was so enormous. The "Dreamboat" era had arrived. These cars had shiny chrome, magnificent upholstery, rounded steel bodywork, and dimensions which drove town planners to distraction. Buick was offering the 144 bhp Roadmaster for 1,895 dollars in 1947, weighed down with 83 pounds (38 kilograms) of chrome trim, and propelled by the silky smooth Dynaflow 3-speed automatic transmission. Unlike the Ford, the 8-cylinder engine fitted lengthwise was a long-stroke in-line engine. Since the mid-1930s, Ford had put all his trust in the V8, and finally, at the beginning of the 1950s, he forced all his main rivals to adopt the same engine layout. This became the typical feature of every genuine American until the beginning of the 1980s.

Chevrolet put their trust in the reliable straight six engines, until, in 1955, customers were introduced to the first V8 engine, the 265 CID with 166 bhp at an extra cost of 250 dollars in the Chevrolet Bel Air. The last American 12-cylinder came off the assembly-line in 1948. This Lincoln Continental ("nothing could be finer") was the first car opened by a push-button door handle. There were no more Lincoln Continentals from Ford until 1956. Ford had long since realized that superfine luxury cars were far less profitable in the short-term than middle-of-the-range cars of the 2,527 dollar Cosmopolitan type, to which cosmetic changes could be made every year. The 1949 price was increased by a

AMERICA IN THE 1940S - BIZARRE SHAPES WITH A HINT OF STREAMLINING WHICH CAUGHT ON

The beginning of the 1940s finally signalled the end of the oversize and overweight classics, such as this massive 1941 Cadillac. Unitized construction bodywork could be manufactured much more cheaply.

whole two dollars for the 1950 model!

At the end of the 1940s, audacious car designers excited the American car world. Mr Preston Tucker is a famous example of an innovator with a few clever ideas which totally baffled the average American citizen. Only 53 of the 1948 Tuckers were built, the "symbol of safety". The ex-aircraft Franklin engine, fitted horizontally in the rear of the car, is an extremely reliable 6-cylinder unit, judging from the 48 cars which are still in existence. The Tucker became famous because of its swivelling centrally-placed third headlight, the 'cyclops eye', which was to illuminate the bends. For the first time, the front passenger had in front of him a thickly padded dashboard. Lack of sufficient capital meant Preston Tucker's dream of the perfect safety car did not materialize.

The Tasco works in Hartford, Connecticut also had ideas which were

The Strout Ford Scarab was built for two years in quite small numbers. President Eisenhower drove a Scarab in France. Its Ford V8 engine was at the rear. The 1949 Nash (above left) was considered a revolutionary streamlined car.

ahead of their time. One of the fascinating features of their Tasco V8 was its almost uninterrupted area of glass giving all-round visibility. Who wants to fry in the summer heat? The firm went bankrupt after producing 12 cars.

The Beech (Beechcraft) aircraft company managed to withdraw from the ruthless car business in time, after an unsuccessful attempt at launching their 1948 Beech Plainsman. An air-cooled aircraft engine drove the many-windowed six-seater, aluminium-panelled automobile. Test drivers felt they were in a rickety sports aircraft shortly before take-off. One sole example found a buyer!

The fate of the highly-praised Airway made by T.P. Hall from San Diego hit the headlines in the Californian press. The unfortunate inventor drove his 10.2 bhp dreamcar off a cliff into the Pacific. At least the Airway was aptly named. The car was driven by a 2-cylinder 4-stroke engine by Onan, which has proved to be one of the best generator engines for yachts to this day.

NEW HEYDAY FOR OLD MODELS OF THE 30S AS 'HOT RODS' OF THE 40S

At the end of the 1940s, the first hot rods appeared on the scene in America. 1930s Ford models were revamped as road-burners with souped-up V8 engines. Here is a Ford series 40, the predecessor to the three-window coupés.

The most famous small car manufacturer in America from 1939 to 1952 was Crosley in Marion, Indiana. Powel Crosley's cute baby car can still be admired today in the Ford museum at Dearborn. It was the American equivalent of the British Morris Minor. For 931 dollars in 1947 and 1948, you could buy a two-seater open sports car with 26 bhp Cobra 4-cylinder engine, or a four-seater sedan or three other versions - a station-wagon, a pick-up or a half-open jeep. Crosley's quality was in no way inferior to the powerful competition in Detroit. But who wants to buy a small car, when for the same money you can buy a big flashy car which is twice the size and far more comfortable? On 31 March 1952, Powel Crosley's accounts were frozen, and the dream of the American small car had again failed to materialize.

In the 1940s, the Big Three in Detroit outdid each other with fulsome advertising slogans which today seem redolent of the whole 'dreamboat' car era. Buick promised their customers in 1947: "When better automobiles are built, Buick will build them". Cadillac responded with "The world's newest engine - for the world's finest cars". Unlike the Ford, the new Cadillac V8 engine was equipped with overhead camshafts and was capable of producing 160 bhp. Cadillac also talked somewhat more modestly of the "Standard of the world".

In 1948, Chrysler, at that time briefly the number 2, created the legendary 'woody' design. The car's wood panelling was so popular with Americans that nearly every Chrysler Town and Country car was decorated with real mahogany and oak until mid-1949. The advertising slogan was worded accordingly - "Be modern - buy Chrysler".

With "There's a finer Ford in your Future", Ford put into words what people wanted to hear. Ford fans were well catered for in 1949, with an 8-cylinder costing 1,517 dollars. Car dealers were particularly pleased with the addition of the overdrive gear, which had to be paid for as an extra. For the first time in the history of the American car industry, the accessory list was so long that the cost of the extras doubled the basic car price. Well-maintained cars of the 1940s are a rarity today. The auction price for rare woodies has long since exceeded the 50,000 dollar mark.

If you go to Istanbul, you can treat yourself to taxi-rides in more or less original Chrysler-built de Sotos, made from 1941 to 1950, and many Chevrolet Bel Airs of the 50s. These long-wheelbase taxis were sold world-wide in the form of seven and eight-seater limousines. These taxis, which are a good 23 ft (7 m) long, are the last survivors from the Dinosaur period of American road cruisers. After 40 years' service and well over a million miles of Turkish roads, Chrysler's apt advertising slogan "The De Soto: Styled to stand out - built to stand up" proved a very accurate description.

Swansong for aristocrats of the road

After the Second World War, the European car industry had difficulty starting up again. Courageous manufacturers like MG took up the challenge: here the TC Midget of 1945-49.

One of the very few technically sophisticated Panhard Dynamic Model 140s is to be found in the motor museum at Ibbenbüren. Central steering, 6 cylinder sleeve valve engine, 80 bhp from 2,861 cc. The clutch is 'preselected' on the gear-shift and engaged with the accelerator pedal.

The Adler type 10. This 2.5 liter, 6-cylinder was sold as the 'Adler Autobahn'. The rear swing-axle and independent front suspension were of the highest technical standard achievable in the 1940s. Its top speed was 80 mph (130 kph)and at 5,750 marks, relatively more expensive car than Opel and Mercedes middle-of-the-range models.

N845

HX-8049
NY HISTORICAL

The Veritas Cabriolet had the new sports car look of 1949. This rare example is from the Ibbenbüren museum. In 1949, the Veritas Scorpion reached over 100 mph (165 kph) with its straight six Heinkel/BMW engine. The designer was Ernst Loof and the space-framed aluminium bodywork was by Spohn. Only about 15 cars were built.

1940
1949

Most German cars of the immediate post-War period were pre-War designs which made a comeback between 1946 and 1950, with a few cosmetic changes. Undisputed favourite was the 1.5 liter Opel Olympia. It also achieved screen fame alongside Hildegard Knef in the film "The Young Sinner".

THE GERMAN FOREST AS FILLING STATION. THE WOOD DISTILLER ERA OF THE 1940S

At the end of the 1930s, the Second World War and Hitler's mad ambitions were not without consequences for the German automobile industry. Company managers had no reason to complain about the shortage of orders - everything was poured into armaments. However, what happened in the area of automobile technological development between 1939 and 1946?

Because of the shortage of liquid fuel, many car drivers screwed an Imbert wood-distilling generator onto their long-suffering Ford Eifel (bottom right). The combination of Ford Eifel and a Detlef caravan made campers' hearts beat faster (bottom left). The streamlined Ford V8 has offbeat looks (above right), while the Type 48 (at the filling station) is sporting and elegant.

Opel, with combined German and American management until 1939, was clearly the number 1 among German motor manufacturers. The reason for its success was well organized, high-volume production on assembly-lines of the unit construction Kadett ('Cadet'), Olympia and Kapitän ('Captain') models. Opel was able to establish itself as the biggest European exporter of cars. The press were ecstatic about the stylish Opel Kapitän with its 55 bhp and a top speed of 80 mph: "a car for all purposes and both sexes". The straight 6-cylinder engine of 2.5 liters impressed by virtue of its good torque and quiet running. At just under 4,000 marks, it had no competitors on the German market. Until 1940, the technically advanced Opel Olympia with a 1.5 liter 4-cylinder engine, was the best-selling German car. This reliable and cheap engine, with minor technical changes, was fitted in the cheaper middle range cars until 1965. The Opel Olympia, with its unmistakable alligator hood - the engine hood could be opened in one piece - was a genuine people's car at the end of the 30s.

The car with the name 'people's car', the Volkswagen, Ferdinand Porsche's most important creation, was converted into a jeep-style vehicle just a few months before the outbreak of war (KdF Type 82). In America, the American Bantam Corporation received a commission to build 70 prototypes of the subsequently legendary Willys Jeep in 49 days. Porsche's KdF and the Willys Overland/Ford jeep were made in greater numbers than any other military cross-country vehicle.

Car production struggled to pick up again in East Germany after the Second World War. This Horch Sachsenring is a rarity from the museum at Oeynhausen. It had a 2.4 liter engine giving 80 bhp and a top speed of about 87 mph (140 kph). There were only 1,382 sixes sold, most of them being the Sachsenring P240.

By the end of the war, 69,000 of the VW equivalent to the jeep had been supplied in its various guises. 600,000 examples of the American jeep were made, excluding those built under license in Russia, Japan and other Pacific countries, some of which to this day, still produce a modified version of the original and are perfectly satisfied with it.

The Second World War consigned a whole series of outstanding designs to the archives. At Daimler-Benz, a 32-unit pre-production run of the Type 600 V/K was produced as late as 1941/42 alongside the full-scale munitions production. Instead of the straight eight M 150 engine (155 bhp or 230 bhp with supercharger), the car (approximately 20 ft or six m long) was fitted with a 6,020 cc V12 engine. Engine performance rose from 170 bhp in the least powerful version to over 240 bhp with a Roots type blower coming in at 3,600 rpm. Not one of these engines, the first twelve-cylinder to be produced in Stuttgart, survived the war, so you will not find one in the Daimler-Benz Museum in Untertürkheim. However, the design drawings have been preserved in a fire-proof safe in the archives.

As in all other countries involved in the war the automobile factories in Germany became exclusively taken up with producing armaments. The victors used this to their advantage. The Auto-Union works were a valuable item on the Soviet occupation forces list of reparations. By mid-1946, the still intact body presses for Horch, Wanderer and DKW had been dismantled and taken to Russia. Production of the modern Opel Olympia and Kadett seemed to offer the best chance of success.

The evergreen Rüsselsheim engine had a happy reincarnation as the 1.5

liter Moskvitsch, which remained in production until the mid-1960s and was exported to all the Iron Curtain countries. In 1948 in the Eastern zone the nationalized IFA concern was created, an amalgamation of the Auto-Union group, BMW in Eisenach, Phänomen in Zittau and other smaller factories in the automobile sector. It was here that the last Horch was built.

THE SLOW DEATH OF THE FRENCH LUXURY CAR

The output of the 1948 Talbot Lago T26 Grand Sport was 240 bhp from 4,483 cc and it easily reached a speed of 130 mph (205 kph). Neither Bugatti, Talbot Lago nor Delahaye survived the rigorous French tax legislation of the 1940s and 1950s.

on which even the most economical Opel Olympia did barely 80 miles (130 kilometers). Necessity is the mother of invention. The Imbert wood-distiller turned out to be a sooty alternative to petrol. Until 1948, whole areas of woodland were sacrificed to keep cars on the road. Woodcutter gangs were hired by Ford and AEG to fuel their own trucks.

After the war, the Western allies considered the idea of one standardized German car. The Volkswagen factory in Wolfsburg was to produce 40,000 of these cars. Ford in Cologne would produce 40,000 trucks, which meant a monopoly for two factories under Allied control. Other car firms were to supply agricultural equipment, refrigerators and similar items. Opel actually produced 5,000 refrigerators per month in 1946, while Daimler-Benz manufactured such items as bicycle trailers, and BMW made saucepans for caterers.

Despite the shortage of materials, over 1,000 VW 'Beetles' per month were rolling off the assembly line in 1946. Only about 30 of them were sold to private owners for coupons, the rest being reserved for the allies. When the worst of the upheaval was over, pre-War cars, which had been carefully stored away, began to appear on the roads again. Most private cars had survived the war relatively well, hidden in haystacks or in holes in the ground. The black market for spare parts and expensive petrol blossomed. Only those with a special authorization were entitled to ten liters of petrol per month,

The recovery of the car industry could not continue like this. The Association of German Engineers (VDI) held a conference in October 1949 on the subject of "The small two-seater as a utility car". From these discussions, the ideal mode of transport for that time took shape in the minds of these engineers - the German mini-car. Without the minicars which later materialized, motorization in Germany would have taken much longer in the 1950s. The engineers required the following specification for a basic model: a 2-cylinder, 2-stroke engine, air-cooled, with a capacity of 400 to 500 cc, 12 to 15 bhp and a fuel consumption of around 60-70 mpg of petroil mixture. Top speed was to be 52 mph, unladen weight 7 cwt or 770 lbs, price around 2,500 marks, two to three seats and a small trunk. It would thus be a mini-car which was about half the price of a VW Beetle, and could be repaired by any motorcycle mechanic because of its technical simplicity.

The VW standard model, costing 4,800 German marks, was an expensive car that only members of the administration or wealthy citizens with good contacts could afford. The resurrected pre-war Mercedes 170V model acquired a diesel variant, the 170D, with the same output of 38 bhp; this model (known in the factory as the 636 4-cylinder), went down in automobile history as the first mass-produced private car with a diesel engine. The 260D, originally introduced prior to the War, was sold almost exclusively for use as taxis. The 636 diesel engine is still being manufactured in Spain, even today, after being in production for more than 50 years, as a reliable industrial and boat engine. The 170V and 170D at 9,200 German marks were nearly twice as expensive as the Volkswagen. Nevertheless, by 1949, a double shift system was set up to cope with the demand. In 1949, the Swabian car manufacturers confounded the experts with the 170S. The car became an icon for the economic miracle of the 1950s. The man in the street was ecstatic about the Mercedes 170S at 10,000 marks, and went on paying the monthly instalments on his Champion 250, costing 2,650 marks. The Gutbrod Superior at 3,990 marks (1950) nevertheless fulfilled higher aspirations.

"IS THERE ANYTHING FURTHER YOU REQUIRE?" EVERY ROLLS-ROYCE WAS CUSTOM-BUILT UNTIL THE 1970S

The first post-War Rolls Royce was this 1946 Silver Wraith. The board of directors thought the 12-cylinder engine from the Phantom III series was too large, in view of the economic situation. Therefore, production was restricted to a development of the pre-War Wraith with a relatively small straight six of only 4.5 liters fitted into the voluminous engine compartment. The entirely handcrafted Silver Wraith was sold in Europe in 1950 for all of 41,000 Swiss francs. Today, a Rolls costs nearly ten times as much.

The extremely light weight construction of these cars allowed one to forget what little traffic there was on cross-country roads. Motorways had been a favourite military target during the war, because they were used as supply lines. Only short stretches of motorway were consequently usable in the late 1940s. Nearly every bridge was destroyed and hardly any motorway tunnels were left intact. Drivers of minicars drove almost permanently at full throttle, but still got to their destination at an average of 40 mph (65 kph). Minicar drivers did not start to complain about the poor performance of their cars until the mid 1950s. In the early days after the War Germans were happy simply to have a roof over their heads.

Among Germany's neighbours, even

Here you can see the difference between a volume production car and the luxurious fittings of a Rolls-Royce. "Comfort never goes out of fashion, and those who have ever driven a Rolls-Royce will remember the pleasure of driving the car for the rest of their lives. This is why it is worth the money" argue Rolls-Royce owners, with some justification.

if statesmen were honored as victors, the ordinary man in England, France and Italy was no better off with his low-budget car than his counterpart in Germany. The English Austin Ten was built almost entirely without modifications from 1937 to 1947 because there was no money for a more modern design. Citroën achieved sales of 700,000 between 1935 and 1956 with its 7CV, the first genuine mass-produced car with front-wheel drive, whereas the 2CV did not become one of the biggest-selling small cars until the mid-1950s.

Italy's Fiat Topolino was probably technically the best small car of the period up to 1955. Compared to the inadequately engined German minicars and the outdated English cars, Fiat plumped for the right mixture. It was a four-seater, with a 4-cylinder engine with water-cooling system, which meant good heating and no overheating problems on hills. Its characteristic shape and its proverbial reliability ensured that the 'mouse' became the best and best-loved small car in post-war Europe.

Hunting Season for the "fast cats"

The Jaguar XK 120 brought a gleam to the eye more than any other sportscar. This is the first series production car with a twin overhead camshaft engine.

BI-AR 275

The 1951 Mercedes 300S provided a direct link with the great luxury cars of the 1930s. It had 175 bhp from a 5,400 cc 6-cylinder fuel-injection engine. Its top speed was around 110 mph (180 kph). Between 1951 and 1958, 760 300S and SC cars were sold at a price of about 34,500 marks. Today it is valued at between 250,000 and 350,000 marks.

The Victoria 250 is one of the 'dream cars' of the 1950s. Electromagnetic five-speed preselected gears, with push-buttons and shift lever on the dashboard. The plastic bodywork was based on an idea of Egon Brütsch. 729 cars of this type were sold between 1957 and 1958, then Victoria went bust.

Although the same coachbuilders turned out either a Rolls-Royce or a Bentley according to demand, the Bentleys of the 40s and 50s were distinguished from the Rolls-Royces by the more sporting gear ratios. This 1959 Bentley S2 is the first model with a V8 engine of 6,230 cc and automatic transmission.

The first Ferrari 250 GTs of 1954 are already valuable rarities today, and fetch top prices at auctions. No other post-War sports car has proved more fascinating than this 12-cylinder of 2,953 cc giving 220 bhp at 7,000 rpm. It was sold until 1966 with a great variety of bodywork styles.

Unlike many other sports car manufacturers, Ferdinand Porsche scored an immediate hit with his first production car, the 356. From 1950 to 1965, the engine's output progressively increased from a tame 40 to 95 bhp. The 2,000 GS Carerra 2 sports racing model even achieved 130 bhp. The 356 C featured here was sold from 1963 to 1965 for around 10,000 to 15,000 dollars. Its present value is around 45,000 dollars.

The Ford Taunus Weltkugel ('Globe'), the big flashy American in a miniature German version. No other middle-of-the-range car had so much chrome trim in 1955 or was so well equipped. This 15 M De Luxe gives 38 bhp and is regarded as a typical product of the German economic miracle.

KÖLN
Ihr Glücksbringer
HOROSKOP
BR 549-656

Sophia Loren, the irresistible beauty from Italy, with her Mercedes 300 SL with its gull-wing doors. Originally designed purely as a sports racing car, the 1954 production version is today the most expensive and most sought-after post-War German sports car at auctions. The gentleman with the 300 SL Roadster is the son of the ex-dictator Trujillo of the Dominican Republic.

Just five years after the end of the Second World War, the world found itself confronted with another war in Korea in June 1950. This substantially hampered the recovery of the European automobile industry. In France, the government ordered a halt to the production of private cars, and in Germany there was an acute shortage of materials. Manufacturers had to be allocated sheet metal for bodies, so that smaller manufacturers had only limited supplies for their customers. At Ford, Opel and Daimler-Benz, delivery for some models was up to two years. Minicar manufacturers improvised with metal sheets welded together and created bodies with them containing many a dent. The essential thing was that production ran more or less to schedule.

At the beginning of the 1950s, faithful miniature versions of the big flashy American cars were praised to the skies by the new automobile magazines. "At first glance, you might think you were looking at a small-scale version of a genuine American car" , declared the "Hamburger Echo" about the new Staunau K 400. Company boss Karl-Heinz Staunau decided to emigrate to South America in February 1951. He

PLASTIC BOMBS OF THE 1950S

They were the stars of the first post-war motor show. Maico 500 Sport (above), with bodywork by Beuttler. The quaint Brütsch-Mopetta, a 50 cc 'egg', that never went into serious production (left). The British Nobel 200 was financed with the help of the Persian Empress Soraya. It was a gigantic flop.

left behind him a state of financial chaos. The Gutbrod Superior 700, despite becoming insolvent in 1954, went down in motoring history as the first passenger car with a fuel injection two-stroke engine. This 2-cylinder, 2-stroke engine, developed by the aircraft company Hirth, was fed the correct mixture direct from the fuel injection pump. A separate lubrication system meant that the Gutbrod Superior 700 E 2-stroke was almost free of any of the usual problems with smelly exhaust or sooty sparking plugs caused by too rich a mixture.

The Gutbrod Superior 700 E with its 30 bhp engine may have won splendid silver trophies for successes in reliability trials, but at 5,750 marks this technically interesting two-seater was 1,000 marks more expensive than the VW Beetle or the new Glas Isar 600/700 and the brilliant NSU Prince 600.

The first post-war Opel Kapitän (Captain) brochure (above left) still shows the pre-War design. The 6-cylinder used American style pontoon construction with unitized bodywork.

The 1950s Opel Rekord treated its owners to a high level of comfort at a reasonable price. The Opel Admiral and Kapitän, which were advertised with the slogan "A car the whole world wants", were very popular with dealers. At that time, no other company in Europe could offer more car for less money.

By the mid-1950s the era of the modest 2-stroke engines was being left behind by developments. Customers now demanded clean 4-stroke engines, five comfortable seats, and a spacious trunk for a frame tent and rubber dinghy. Camping became the craze of the 1950s. "Pack die Badehose ein" (Pack your swimming costumes) trilled Conny Froboess.

In July 1953, Volkswagen celebrated the production of the 500,000th 'Beetle'. 19,000 factory workers and office employees had the opportunity of winning 600 bicycles, 40 motorcycles and 5 'Beetles' in a kind of roulette game. 1,000 'Beetles' per day rolled off the assembly line in 1953. The Messerschmitt factory in Regensburg regarded their new KR 175 cabin scooter, as the "jet fighter of the ordinary man". "ADAC Motorwelt" (the journal of the motoring organization), said at the time "The basic concept of a cabin scooter is absolutely right." In that same year of 1953, the ultra-rapid Mercedes 300 SLE was developed in Stuttgart-Untertürkheim. USA importer Maxie Hoffmann pressed for mass production and immediately placed an order for 1,000 cars.

The new Ford Taunus Weltkugel ('Globe') won the hearts of middle-class Germans, and delivery times increased to nine months. In an effort to soothe angst-ridden passengers, Opel gave rear-seat passengers acute sea-sickness with their softly sprung Opel Olympia Rekord. "An American car for Germany" said the "Hamburger Abendblatt" (the Hamburg evening newspaper) in praise of the new design, and swore that "Never had driving a motor car been such a pleasure as in this middle-of-the-range luxury car".

In 1953, one in every fifty Germans drove a private car. Twice as many French owned such cars as a Renault 4CV, Citroen 2CV or 7CV. One in four American people already had a car. Six years later, statistically speaking, every American was driving his own car. The endless stream of traffic was rolling progressively faster towards the chaos we know today as modern traffic.

Dawn of the new classics America's dream cars

This Skylark convertible was launched on the occasion of Buick's 50th jubilee in 1953. In terms of sales, the Skylark proved to be a lame duck. Today, it is worth well over half a million dollars.

PARK AVENUE
"It's long, low and lovely!"
"Everything about it says quality!"
New Quality-Built Bodies bring new beauty and safety to the low-price field! They're longer! They're wider! They're stronger! They come in the widest variety of body style, color and upholstery combinations of any low-priced car.
Coast to coast success... it's the
Ablest car on the American Road...'52 Ford!
CALIFORNIA ST.
"Ford's Strato-Star V-8 whisks you up hills in a wink!"
New Power—Six or V-8. The newest, most modern Six! It has free-turning overhead valves and it's the only all-new, low-friction, high-compression Six in the industry. Ford's high-compression Strato-Star V-8—now 110-h.p.—is the most powerful engine in its field!
MESA VERDE TRAIL
"Dust, drafts, discomfort are 'has beens' when you hit the trail!"
"And no 'jingle jangle' on rough dirt roads!"
New Automatic Ride Control really "gentles" the bumps! And a new lower center of gravity and a wider front tread help take the tilt out of turns!
PENNSYLVANIA AVE.
"Forward or backward you get broad vision all the time!"
"Nips in and out of tight parking places in a jiffy!"
New Full-Circle Visibility really "lets in" all the scenery! You'll find a huge, curved one-piece windshield, a car-wide rear window, narrower posts all around... side windows that are picture-window big. Here's visibility unlimited!
You can pay more but you can't buy better!
1952
White sidewall tires, if available, optional at extra cost. Equipment, accessories and trim, subject to change without notice.

Some shapes are unforgettable, like this 1950 Ford Mercury. In its day it was a resounding flop, but now it is a sought-after classic. "Nothing like it on the road" was how Ford advertised the Mercury, but the following year they launched it with a totally new body.

This 1953 Buick Roadmaster was expertly restored at great expense by Elmo Classic in Stuttgart. Value more than 500,000 dollars. Dynaflow 3-speed automatic gear box. A gear shift on the steering column. 188 bhp, V8 engine, four-barrel carburetor.

Contemporary taste in the mid-1950s led many car fans to take up metal shears and welding apparatus themselves. This prize-winning tail-finned monster was produced in 1959. Studebaker embarked on a radical break-away from the tail-fin design with the Avanti (below) - a courageous but unsuccessful attempt to swim against the tide of contemporary taste.

This was also typical of the spirit of the 1950s: an underwater hotel in Florida. The bar and saloon were located beneath the waterline, until a guest drew a pistol at the sight of a blue marlin.

FAP·820
COLORADO

Marilyn Monroe owned 3 Ford Thunderbirds. This 1957 V8 Model E packs a solid 285 bhp, and easily reaches a top speed of 140 mph (220 kph). A real 'Thunderbird' of its day. Its value today is around 45,000 dollars.

Beautifully styled engineering design became increasingly popular at the end of the 1950s. Here is a heavily chromed Jaguar rear axle with inboard disc brakes. Jaguar was the first car firm to fit disc brakes as standard equipment.

Two Chevrolet Corvettes. The blue 1954 Corvette, still with a straight 6-cylinder engine giving 150 bhp, was decidedly underpowered. Today's value about 72,000 marks. The red 1959 Corvette, with a 270 bhp V8 engine and 4-speed manual transmission; a rival for the Mercedes 300SL. This car belongs to Princess Gloria von Thurn und Taxis.

Fuel Injection

The large six-seater convertibles - this is a 1957 Oldsmobile Golden Rocket - were sold for a song in their day. 2,691 dollars bought 277 bhp. That was 300 dollars more than for the hardtop sedan.

CALIFORNIA
MONTH
YEAR
2CZA061
The Golden State

Every American knows the 1957 Chevrolet Nomad Bel Air. Chrome trim covered the body of one of the most attractive and successful vehicles of the fifties. The Nomad could rightly claim that it was not only a fully fledged dreamboat of a car, but also a practical utility vehicle. Ford and Plymouth were unable to challenge its success.

Publicity men searched for impressive names even in the fifties. This 1957 Chevrolet Bel Air Convertible had the new 'Triple Turbine Turboglide' - a simple 3-speed automatic transmission with an emergency low gear.

100
110
INSIDE AIR
OUTSIDE AIR
TEMP

GHS 989

CALIFORNIA
63
GHS 989

Technically, the Cadillac is still considered to be the best American luxury car. Only 532 of this 1953 Eldorado Convertible were built It is valued today at 62,500 dollars. It had a 5.6 liter engine giving 210 bhp. The 'Autronic Eye' caused the headlights to dip automatically at night when a car approached.

At the end of the fifties, the price of petrol still played a very minor role. Consequently sports cars and tuned stock cars used "gas-guzzling" engines. This one has 8 cylinders, a supercharger and an output of about 400 bhp.

1950
1959

The fifties. The beginning of a new era for the USA. Dazzling prospects for all Americans. At last there was money to spend on exciting rock 'n' roll records and hula hoops, and even enough dollars to buy cars with tail-fins. Petticoats and jeans with studs replaced the nice-girl-good-boy look. The pre-War generation were confronted with a totally new lifestyle. The decade produced heroes and villains, losers and winners in unheard of numbers. It is not only the idols and events of that era which exert a special fascination on us today, but also the shiny chrome-plated beauties on four wheels, which transport us back to a time that is an inspiration to the youth of today. An invasion of chrome and steel swept over America in the fifties. A two-and-a-half ton car for just 2,500 dollars.

"Styling and glamour in place of sophisticated technology and good handling". This was how German test drivers assessed the legendary battleships of the jukebox era. Not surprising - they had little time for extreme luxury and extravagant styling at the beginning of the fifties. No doubt envy contributed in part to these judgements. After all, they had lost the War, and the German car firms, only just back on their feet, were glad of all the custom they could muster.

Turkish Dodge seven-seater of 1951. The Dodge was produced under license in the Far East and in Asia by local car firms.

BUILT TO LAST FOR EVER? MANY BIG FLASHY AMERICAN CARS ARE STILL ON THE GO AFTER EARNING THEIR LIVING FOR 50 YEARS ON TURKISH ROADS.

Given proper care and attention, American cars will last an eternity. The Chrysler (above) has more than a million miles (2 million kilometers) to its credit. The massive 1939 De Soto (below) - with the speedometer disconnected - has already fed three generations of a Turkish cab driver's family.

With hindsight we can see that American mass-produced cars of that era were excellent practical cars for the right markets. Opinions are divided on technical qualities, but one thing is certain: fifties' American cars have established themselves quite high up on the list of collectors' favorites.

Since the last stock market crash in the autumn of 1987, it has become painfully clear to many financial wizards that under certain circumstances you will get a quicker return on your investment if you put your money into high-class classic cars, than if you invest it on the stock market in bad times.

At an American auction it was demonstrated that a Bugatti Royale, built in 1930 for around 45,000 dollars, is today worth 20 million dollars. In 1998, this super-classic, of which only six examples were made, should fetch 75 million dollars, according to the estimate of auctioneer Dean Kruse.

But there are even more astounding examples. In 1962, the last front-engined Ferrari 330 GTO was rolled out of the hallowed halls of Modena. It was the last Ferrari that was capable of setting long-distance records as a standard production car, coming second and third at Le Mans in 1962. Just 24 years later, this car was sold for

It brought tears to everyone's eyes. A lady with a white poodle on leopard-skin seat covers in the 1958 Oldsmobile. The flying car is a 1951 Convair-Studebaker. This firm manufactured five different flying cars which are today regarded as great rarities.

Fortunately, this fifties' dream car with the sad-eyed headlights was to experience an uncertain future (1956 General Motors Futura).

9,268,000 francs (1,875,000 dollars) at an auction in Monaco. A 1958 250 Testarossa, however, fetched a remarkable 1,625,000 dollars. Both cars were sold for just under 62,500 dollars, in 1958 and 1963 respectively, to customers in the world of motor sport. Their increase in value corresponds to a profit of thirty times their original value -a remarkable return on investment. The market for top-quality classic cars experienced a boom in the USA, which by European standards was hardly credible. In 1955, 185,000 big flashy Chevrolet Bel Air hardtops rolled off the assembly line at General Motors. Each cost 2,067 dollars. Today, the finest examples would fetch 12,000 to 15,000 dollars at auction. Auctioneer Rick Cole estimates the number of roadworthy cars to be 150,000. By 1998, their value should be at least 50,000 dollars.

Prices for the real rarities are increasing at a substantially faster rate.

This 1957 Studebaker Golden Hawk was way ahead of its time. It had 275 bhp and the bodywork was by the famous designer Raymond Loewy. The Golden Hawk was obviously too small for contemporary tastes.

THE SENSATION FROM AMERICA - THE 1956 FORD FAIRLINE-MONTEREY

German car test drivers gaped when they saw genuine big American dreamboats at Ford in Cologne. They had 225 bhp V8 engines and suspension like a double bed.

A 1948 Tucker, which could once be acquired for 2,485 dollars, today costs 100,000 dollars, and by 1998 should fetch 350,000 dollars. Preston Tucker only sold 51 cars. The present number of survivors stands at 48.

The value of particularly fine American classic cars from the forties to the sixties is also shooting up even in Germany. Market leader Elmo Classic in Stuttgart is today selling expensively restored big American dreamboats from 60,000 to way over 100,000 marks (37,500 to 65,000 dollars). A Chevrolet Nomad costs around 70,000 marks (43,750 dollars), and a 1963 Chevrolet Corvette split-window was sold for over 81,000 marks (50,625 dollars).

Conversely, a Mercedes-Benz 300 SL light-alloy coupé can sell for 350,000 to 400,000 marks (220,000 to 250,000 dollars) to a (Japanese) businessman. These were unthinkable prices a couple of years ago. Today, the charisma and quality of the car determine the price.

Bentleys, Lamborghinis and numerous Porsche 356s are on offer, but it is the classic car market in

American models which is booming. "Jumping on the bandwagon happens in all trades. There are, of course, some dealers who try to acquire a share of the market with badly restored cars. As the saying goes, there's a boom in scrap metal again".

Compared to European saloons of the fifties, the American models of this era were lavishly equipped with extras which play a decisive role in their value today. Hydraulically operated window lifters and push-button operated cabrio roofs are difficult when spare parts are needed. A push-button radio using valves today costs over 1.250 dollars and is faithfully repaired by good restorers. The multi-colored leather upholstery of luxurious interiors cannot be repaired with German leather.

Wolfgang Sälzler, Managing Director of Elmo Classic, put it this way, "American engines and transmissions last much longer than the bodywork. A car from New York is of no interest to us, but a car from the heat of Colorado or even from Chile is of interest. Certain cars and their spare parts are so rare, that it is pointless trying to restore them. Anyone offering a car like that in Germany cannot be trustworthy, because he has certainly not used original parts for the restoration work." What are future trends likely to be? The car must have character. Its future value will also hinge on whether and how far its appeal coincides with prevailing taste. For the really wealthy customers it is of no consequence whether the car costs 100,000 or 200,000 dollars. The deciding factors are the mechanical condition and pristine outward appearance. Sälzler continued: "If a customer discovers an Opel exhaust system on a 1949 Ford Mercury, the deal is off. Therefore, it is absolutely pointless cutting corners with restoration work. A good restoration firm will specialise in only a few models."

Daimler-Benz, for example, has some of their Grand Prix racing cars restored in England, because the English have specialists who are experts on pre-War racing engines. A senior employee explained, "The technical expertise is so good there. Otherwise, it would mean using our best people, and they are needed elsewhere on bigger projects". The ever rising labour costs and increasingly high standard of work demanded by clients are causes of today's exorbitantly high prices for exceptional cars in the luxury category.

A 12-cylinder Maybach Zeppelin was auctioned in Hamburg at the end of 1988 for 650,000 marks (406,250 dollars). This is considered to be a tremendously high price. At Rick Cole's Pebble Beach auction, an almost identical Maybach was sold for 600,000 dollars (at the current rate of exchange). "The car is a pure investment" said Rick Cole, "In two years, the Maybach will have driven 200 miles, and will fetch 750,000 to 800,000 dollars, because in the whole of America there are fewer than five 12 cylinder Maybachs."

Competition between Japanese and American buyers is giving further impetus to prices. The sky's the limit. European car freaks still seem to be fascinated by the technical perfection of old cars, while in the USA the craze is for playing for soaring returns on investment at auctions. Wolfgang Sälzler continued, "Big bucks start at 1 million dollars. Before the auction, less well-known bidders have to submit a certified bank statement to the auctioneer. Fictitious transactions do not take place in America. Raising your finger can mean shelling out millions of dollars. In future, therefore, there will be two classes of classic car fans. Europeans love the beautiful engineering and Americans and Japanese the lovely money that it brings in."

THE BIG DREAMBOAT CARS OF THE FIFTIES - NEVER WAS THERE MORE HORSE-POWER FOR LESS MONEY.

Fresh air rushes past the headlights and on into the interior of this 1957 Chevrolet Bel Air. For a few dollars more or less, the customer could choose between the 140, 185, 245 and 283 bhp versions. This red 1957 Bel Air cost 2,464 dollars.

General Motors chief stylist Harley Earl is reputed to be the inventor of the tail-fin era. It was on the 1955 Cadillac Eldorado Biarritz that the rear wings stuck up sharply for the first time. By 1961, the whole craze was over. Above left and main picture: the 1958 380 bhp Chrysler Windsor. The late fifties radiator grille was called the pancake design. By today's standards, a distinct lapse of taste.

The new classic! There are only 1,285 examples of this 1960 Cadillac Eldorado Biarritz Convertible. Valued today at around 62,500 dollars. 6.3 liters, 345 bhp, 19 ft (5.78 m) long. A gigantic finned car. The 'dream-boat' cars that came after it were progressively smaller. A rare piece of automobile history.

Time flies past. This 1963 Chevrolet Corvette split-window coupé today fetches top prices. The retractable headlights, central locking for the wheels, and the new 5.3 liter V8 fuel injection engine giving 360 bhp were considered sensational technology. Performance-wise, this Stingray was streets ahead of the competition.

Index
The numbers in brackets denote illustrations

Transedition Books would like to thank the following: Reinhard Lintelmann; the Norddeutsche Auto-und Motorradmuseum and the Veteranenfahrzeughof; the Auburn-Cord-Duesenberg Museum; Uschi Danjek; the Historisches Archiv; Ion Zamfirescu; Bodo Fischer and the Alt-Opel-Vereinigung Wolfgang Sälzler.

Photographs: Daimler-Benz AG Historisches Archiv: frontispiece, pp 10-11, p34, pp70-71, pp75-76, p152; Duesenberg Museum USA: pp46-47, pp50-52; Elmo Classic/Gaukler Studios GmbH, Stuttgart: pp6-7, pp8-9, p115 (top), pp119-120, p156, pp162-163, pp166-167, pp170-171, p178, pp189-190, pp191-192, back cover; Ford AG, Cologne: p23 (right), p26 (top left), pp 28-29; The Kobal Collection/New Eyes GmbH/edition cicero GmbH, fine art publishers, Hamburg: p166; Reinhard Lintelmann, Espelkamp: pp12-13, pp14-15, pp24-25, pp30- 31, pp78-79, p80, pp88-90, pp91-92, pp93-94, pp98-100, p102, p103 (centre), pp126-127, pp143-135, pp136-137, pp138-139, pp140-141, pp144-145; Philip Morris AG, Munich: p9, pp158-160, pp168-169, pp172-173, p180-181; OPEL AG Rüsselsheim: p132, pp154-155, p184 (bottom left); Renault historic archives, Paris: p28 (bottom left), p63, (top right); H J Richter/MOT-Stuttgart: p135 (right); Rothändle-Raritäten-Show: pp16-17, pp85-86, p96. All other photographs: Hans Georg Isenberg, Fellbach Graphic design: Herbert Emmer, Asemwald/Stuttgart and Wolfgang Kelling, Stuttgart. Jacket Picture: National Motor Museum, Beaulieu, England.

Translation: Christine Bainbridge in association with First Edition Translations Ltd, Cambridge.

Printed in Slovenia

Published in Germany in 1989 by Falken Verlag GmbH, Niedernhausen/Ts.
This edition published in the UK in 1993 by Transedition Books, 11-15 The Vineyard, Abingdon, Oxon OX14 3PX, England.

ISBN 1 898250 00 6